I0554774

A Journey of Faith & Courage

A Woman's Struggle Through Illness & Depression

Sophia McCray

Edited by
Nicole Queen

I dedicate this book to my two boys Ellijah and Josiah McCray. It is because of you both that I survived. You boys are my rock. You held my hand in the dark and brought me into the light. Although our road was not easy, you've shown me God's grace, kindness, mercy, and respect as your mother. What seemed to be trials and stumbles to us, were blessings in disguise.

Grace for the Journey

Dear God,

I am in awe of Your splendor and wondrous love. I love the way You love me. Thank You for what You have bestowed upon me, even those things that I didn't understand while going through this journey of life.

Father God, I need You to come into my life now and help me surrender to You all my hurt and pain that holds me from the blessings of my future. Please help me release the demons of contempt and rejection from my heart, the anger and pain from my soul, and the umbrella of neglect that hovers from them both.

Please forgive me, Father, as I recognize that all of my help comes from You, My Lord. You are all I need. Shape me, Lord, so that I may move closer to You spiritually and emotionally.

Sprinkle me with patience so that I may wait in silence and listen for Your voice to lead me in the right direction.

Father God, I give You an all-access pass to my heart. I pray this in Your most gracious and holy Name, Christ Jesus. *Amen.*

And so, my journey begins...

Contents

Introduction

*"But he was wounded for our transgressions, he was
bruised for our iniquities: the chastisement of
our peace was upon him; and with his stripes we
are healed."*

— Isaiah 53:5 KJV

No one ever thinks that God's plans for their life will be challenging— at least not until something life-changing happens. I remember the exact date when my life changed. It was March 31, 2007. I went to school and taught 6th grade that day. I wasn't feeling well all week. At the time, I was 22½ weeks pregnant. I had been to the doctor earlier in the week to discuss this uncomfortable pain I was having. I wasn't sure how to describe it or even exactly where it was, but it was intense. We thought it was trapped gas. *Yes, gas!* If you've ever been pregnant, you know that you have had either indigestion or horrible gas, and it can be most embarrassing, to say the least!

On that fateful day, my students knew that I was extremely uncomfortable, so they were perfect angels. However, 3:30 pm could not come any sooner for me. I signed out my older son Ellijah, who was in first grade at that time, and home we went. I knew I had to bake him a bunny cake for the Easter parade the next day, so I got right to it. While the cake was cooling, the symptoms persisted. So, I sent him up to my mom's room and told her I needed to rest. I tried everything, even begging God for His mercy on me and our baby.

That evening, while I laid naked on the floor in a fetal position, I had an out-of-body experience. I saw myself standing over myself, watching as I lay on the floor, passed out from the pain. I was crying. The next thing I realized, I was in the hospital, going in and out of consciousness. The stench of the hospital made me nauseous, and the wretched pain took over my body, as I was screaming uncontrollably. My husband sat worried, wondering what was wrong with his wife. *What is happening?*

During this time, we both were saved Christians. We went to church occasionally, lived by the Word of God, but we did not seek Him diligently. We didn't go to church regularly or belong to a church. *Have you ever been negligent in your walk with God? Have you ever fallen off the horse? Have you ever not been as diligent as you should be in your reading and understanding of the Word of God?* Don't worry; it's okay. You're not in trouble. God will never leave you or forsake you.

> *"Fear not, for I have redeemed you; I have called you by name; you are mine. When you pass through the waters, I will be with you, and through the*

rivers, they will not overwhelm you. When you walk through the fire, you will not be scorched or burned, nor will the flame kindle upon you."

— Isaiah 43:1b-2 KJV

If you've ever found yourself in this position, now is a good time for reflection. Reflect on the character of Jesus. *Does He not exhibit love, joy, peace, patience, kindness, goodness, faithfulness, gentleness, and self control?* Your situation may seem bleak and appear like He's not listening, but I assure you, He is. He already knows what you are going through. God knows your heart. He's just waiting for your correct response to your situation.

"Notwithstanding she shall be saved in childbearing, if they continue in faith and charity and holiness with sobriety."

— 1 Timothy 2:15 KJV

O Lord my God,
I cried unto
thee, and thou
hast healed me.

PSALM 30:2 KJV

Chapter 2 Theme

2 "I am the *rose of *Sharon,
The *lily of the valleys."

2 "Like a lily among the thorns,
So is *my darling among the *maidens."

3 "Like an *apple tree among the trees of the forest,
So is my beloved among the *young men.
In his shade I took great delight and sat down,
And his *fruit was sweet to my *taste.

4 "He has *brought me to *his *banquet hall,
And his *banner over me is love.

5 "*Sustain me with *raisin cakes,
Refresh me with *apples,
Because I am *lovesick.

6 *His *left hand is under my head,
And his *right hand embraces me.

7 "I *adjure you, O *daughters of Jerusalem,
By the *gazelles or by the *hinds of the field,
That you do not *arouse or awaken my *love
Until she pleases.

Healing Through Pain

After what seemed like several hours, the doctors came back to tell my husband that they must do emergency surgery. They were not able to find the problem, so they needed to go in and look. They told my husband that there was a high possibility that he would lose us both. However, they informed him that they had to move fast in order to try to save at least one of us. After hearing this devastating news, my husband signed for consent and we prayed. Intense pain took over my entire body, causing me to beg for help. I was so scared. I cried because of my heartache and body ache. The thought of losing my baby or myself was too much to bear. I closed my eyes and exhaled, asking God to deliver me from it all.

Upon waking up in recovery, I was told that I had a ruptured appendix and that my baby saved my life. He had pinched my appendix, which caused the poison to slowly ooze out— just enough to affect me, but not him. And by God's grace, effects were not enough to kill either of us. The doctors couldn't believe it. There was an amazing story about my baby and me going around the hospital, and how we both survived such an ordeal. God showed us great mercy and love. He knew we were His children and He never left our side. And although that was the first time, God wasn't through with me yet.

After surgery, I was taken to the maternity ward for observation. This was the beginning of my healing process, so I thought. The following Saturday after the surgery, I started walking to the bathroom on my own. Upon relieving myself, I had an explosion of blood and fluid come out of me, dispersing all over the cold, hospital floor. I was so scared. I immediately thought, "My baby!" So, I pulled the emergency cord and staff came running. They carried me back to my bed and called my doctors to my bedside. The surgeon pulled up my gown, only to see that my insides were fully exposed! The wound had dehisced. My stomach was wide open. My doctor had his hand inside of my stomach, trying to put my bowels back in! *Gross, right?* Imagine what I thought! My doctor pressed the code blue button. I thought that code blue meant death, so I was worried! As I was laying there, a rush of emergency doctors and nurses flooded my room and began preparing me for emergency surgery. Due to the urgency, I was unable to call my husband to tell him what was going on.

As they placed a cold, foil-like sheet over me, I began to question God's plan for my life. *What's going on here?* We cannot possibly go through another surgery! The last one was risky, enough. *What am I doing wrong? Why are You punishing me?*

Just because we are Christians does not mean we are exempt from pain or trials. This may sound ridiculous, and please forgive me if it does, but sometimes, I think the pain we experience may be worse, so that we can set an example for others regarding how to react and lead others to Christ.

> *Surely he hath borne our griefs, and carried our*
> *sorrows: yet we did esteem him stricken, smitten*
> *of God, and afflicted.*
>
> — Isaiah 53:4 KJV

Most of the time, it takes a tragedy to lead sinners to Christ. Yes, we have a human side. And sometimes, we may cry and struggle. But in the end, it's our spiritual side that wins, and God prevails! We show others how to communicate with God. With prayer and supplication, you can ask God for forgiveness and receive Him in your heart. You can ask for God's love and He will love you back. How good it is to praise His Name! In good times and bad, shout His name and thank Him for waking you up. When we love and trust Him with everything, we bring His heart so much joy! Loving and trusting Him also brings us an abundance of peace.

> *Don't worry about anything; instead, pray about*
> *everything. Then you will experience God's*
> *peace, which exceeds anything we can*
> *understand.*
>
> — Philippians 4:6-7 KJV

Once again, God brought us to it and He brought us through it. He was not through with me yet! Following my emergency surgery, I continued my journey of healing, once again. I was moved to a regular ward, and made steady progress— until several days later.

On April 22, 2007, I began cramping in my lower back, legs, and stomach. I knew this was the beginning of labor, but I also knew that it was way too early. I told the nurse about my pain, and was put on bed rest. I informed about the importance of keeping the baby in. Early delivery proposed serious risk and possible death. I was barely 27 weeks and the baby was about 1 lb 10 oz. The doctor gave me a medicine called Pitocin to stop my labor; however, God's plan was unstoppable.

Man can never hold a candle to what God has planned for you and your life. Sometimes, we forget that He already knows what the problem is because He wrote our destiny. He just wants you to realize that He knows and for you to share your heart with Him in your prayers. Let Him in. Allow Him to take full control. Let go and let God be almighty in your life!

*And let us not be weary in doing well: for in due
season we shall reap if we faint not.*

— Galatians 6:9 KJV

On April 24, 2007, "King" Josiah Alvin McCray was born at 10:40 AM. He was breached and weighed 1 lb 10 oz. Because I recently had staples in my stomach, I had to vaginally deliver him. Having a C-section was too dangerous for us both, as we had already undergone two previous surgeries. Josiah came into the world crying.

God is so good. In that moment, I knew that He had amazing plans for Josiah's life. They briefly showed me my son to, and then whisked him away to the Neonatal Intensive Care

Unit. My husband was so proud of me and happy to see our son. As he held me, I knew we were going to be alright.

I did not get to see Josiah for a couple of hours, as I had to heal, as well. I did not know what to expect. He was so small and frail. I could see every bone in his body, including his heartbeat. The wires and monitors echoed in my head like loud drums playing offbeat tunes. I wanted to kiss and hold him, but I couldn't. I had a whirlwind of emotions. I had so much learning to do. *What about my son, Ellijah? How is he going to feel? And what about my husband; how will he manage with me being absent so long? Can I really do this with my body being so weak?* Despite the questions, I quickly realized that with God as my anchor, anything is possible.

Reflection Questions

1. Name three things that you learned from this chapter.

_____

_____

_____

_____

_____

2. What did this chapter reveal about your walk with Jesus Christ?

_____

_____

_____

_____

_____

3. What scriptures from this chapter resonate in your heart? How can they bring transformation to your life?

_____

_____

_____

_____

_____

Prayer of Rebirth

I invite you to pray the following prayer with me in faith.

God, despite my failures, I wholeheartedly believe that You are with me, encouraging me not to give up. Please help me to remember that with Your help, I can do all things. I'm just a passenger on this ride. I submit all of my anxieties and fears to You, My God, as You are in control. In the Name of Jesus, I pray. Amen.

Beloved. I wish above all things that thou mayest prosper and be in health. even as thy soul prospereth.

3 JOHN 1:2 KJV

17 "The beams of our houses are ...
Our rafters, ... cypresses.

Chapter 2 Theme

2 "I am the rose of Sharon,
The lily of the valleys."

2 "Like a lily among the thorns,
So is my darling among the maidens."

3 "Like an apple tree among the trees of the forest,
So is my beloved among the young men.
In his shade I took great delight and sat down,
And his fruit was sweet to my taste.

4 "He has brought me to his banquet hall,
And his banner over me is love.

5 "Sustain me with raisin cakes,
Refresh me with apples,
Because I am lovesick.

Healing Through Hardship

Over the next several months, Josiah and I went through a series of medical challenges. Explaining things to Ellijah was difficult. He was a very strong boy, although extremely worried about his younger brother.

Josiah was born with two holes in his heart. Because of that, we had to spend some time at Boston Children's Neonatal Unit. The two holes in his heart caused serious blood infections. In addition, my healing process was compromised due to Josiah's infection. As a result, I was admitted to Boston's Brigham Women's Hospital. Therefore, my husband traveled back and forth between the two of us. I was so blessed and proud to call him my husband. Truly, God was responsible for his strength.

The Lord is their strength, and he is the saving
strength of his anointed. Save thy people, and

bless Thine inheritance: feed them also, and lift them up forever.

— Psalm 28:8-9 KJV

After spending two weeks in Boston, we progressed well enough to return home to our hospital in Bermuda. We stayed there until July 3, 2007. Our time had finally come to go home.

At first, it was rough caring for such a small child. Josiah was only 4 lbs when he was released, and I was also still weak. Everyone was so happy to see us. It was truly the work of God that led us to that very moment. The only thing I didn't know was that God was just preparing me for what was really to come. He wanted me to come in all the way— not one foot in the door and the other one out. He wanted me front and center, with both feet in. Where He was about to take me required me to stay directly in His presence on my knees, as only He could deliver me from what was to come.

This was the season for me to stop acting and to start doing. Never in my wildest dreams did I imagine that my life would have taken such turns. God gave me so much to be thankful for. But suddenly— just like that— it was gone!

God has such a funny sense of humor. Sometimes, I think He wants us to get a reality check. Well, then— *checkmate*!

September came, and before I knew it, we made the decision to move back to the USA. It was something we planned, but didn't expect to move as early as we'd thought. My husband desired to go home to be closer to his daughter, as she was having difficulty and needed her dad. So, away we went! Money was tight and things were rough. We needed to hold things together in order to make it. We lived with his parents, so certain rules applied.

Soon after the move, my health began to quickly decline. I wasn't completely healed from having two previous surgeries, so any additional pain was a major discomfort. First, the pain struck me in my legs and hips. Then, I experienced cramping and burning all over my skin. I felt like I was on fire! I could not sleep, and anything that touched my body caused further inflammation. It was the most brutal pain I'd ever felt. It even hurt to walk. I couldn't go to a doctor because we didn't have insurance; we had no money and my green card had not yet arrived. My husband didn't secure new employment yet. I was in a tailspin of pain and had no clue what to do.

Whosoever shall call on the name of the Lord shall be delivered.

—Joel 2:32a KJV

Another month went by, and the pain escalated. I was having trouble breathing. I couldn't even read my kids a bedtime story without coughing and losing breath. It began to get really scary. My husband had just found work and God's mercy was upon us. We received medical insurance and I was finally able to schedule a doctor's appointment.

Towards the beginning of our journey, we didn't seek God diligently. However, when we moved, we were comfortable and ready to head deep into His Word. We were faithful members at Mount Vernon United Methodist Church. After all, God had shown us so much love and mercy; He deserved honor, praise, love, and glory. As we honored Him, my sickness grew worse. I began to wonder if I was being punished for not seeking Him when I should have years ago. *What did I do so wrong to deserve such pain?* I made myself remember how faithful God had been all this time and calmness came over me. I quietly spoke:

> *But my God shall supply all [my needs] according to*
> *His riches in glory by Christ Jesus.*
>
> — Philippians 4:19 KJV

When I went to the doctor, she was taken back by my symptoms. After completing several blood tests, she believed I had lupus and suggested that I see a rheumatologist for confirmation. She referred me to a doctor at George Washington University Hospital. I heard rave reviews about their care and was eager to to get my much needed answers.

On the day of my appointment, I was nervous. I conducted my research and discovered that there was nothing good about lupus. Everything led to death. I felt like I was walking the plank! I felt like I needed to get my affairs in order. Wait! What affairs? We just moved here; we didn't plan for this! I don't even have life insurance! What about my kids? They need their mommy! I found myself screaming inside of my head. To shake me back into reality, I heard my name being called. I stood slowly and walked down the empty hallway, which echoed like the walk of doom. I sat in the office and the nurse took my blood pressure, weight, and temperature. I had a fever and my blood pressure was too high. That, already, was cause for concern. The tech finished her pre-assessment and told me the doctor would be right in. As I sat waiting I looked around at the certificates and photos that marked the walls. I could see the doctor was very accomplished, so that put me at ease. The doctor came in shortly after. She was of Native American descent, extremely kind, and soft-spoken. She immediately addressed my previous blood work and ordered some of her own.

Then, we talked about my pain and symptoms. She suggested that I see a pulmonologist for my breathing issues and to immediately have a CT scan of my chest to check for any damage to my lungs. Then, she confirmed the diagnosis of lupus with an overlap of what she thought may be scleroderma.

After looking at the condition of my hands, she also confirmed that I had a serious condition called Raynaud's Disease, which resulted in poor circulation of blood in my hands and feet. My knuckles were covered in painful ulcers that looked like they were ready to burst.

At the conclusion of the visit, she asked if I had any questions. I told her that I would ask them once the results came back. I was too shaken and my mind was too scattered to ask at that time. To make me a bit more comfortable, she prescribed a steroid called Prednisone. She said that she would start me at 100 mg and may have to go up, depending on the results. She informed me that it would help with inflammation, which was one thing she was sure I had plenty of.

I left the appointment feeling overwhelmed and scared. "Wow lupus," I thought, "what am I going to do now?"

> *The humble will see their God at work and be glad.*
> *Let all who seek God's help be encouraged.*
>
> — Psalm 69:32 KJV

Before going back to the doctor appointment, I decided to apply for employment. We barely made ends meet, and I knew my husband could use my help. He never said it, but his demeanor changed as his stress level went up. So, I waited in prayer, asking God to have mercy on my soul.

I was successful in getting hired as a data entry clerk at a non-profit organization. The pay was good and the benefits were great! It was such a blessing that it was seasonal, as I was able to be home with the kids.

A week later, my phone rang and the doctor wanted to see me, immediately. I was scared to hear the results of all the tests that came back in. So, I just sat quietly at my desk at work in distress, as the tears burned my face. Crying in my cubicle was not cool. I hoped no one would see or hear me. I didn't know what to do or how to feel.

On my way to the doctor, my head raced with disturbing thoughts. *What do I do if the news is bad?* There I go again, not trusting God in the process.

When I reached the office, I went in and said a quick prayer over myself:

God, thank You for waking me up today. Another day to give you joy, gives my heart joy. Father, You are in charge of the report. You are a great physician. You have the final say and I choose You over it all. I quiet my heart and my head so that no matter what I hear today, above all, I hear you. Amen.

For the Word of God is quick, and powerful, and
sharper than any two-edged sword, piercing
even to the dividing asunder of soul and spirit,
and of the joints and marrow, and is a discerner
of the thoughts and intents of the heart.

— Hebrews 4:12 KJV

During the visit, the doctor confirmed the diagnosis, and explained that a person with both lupus and overlapping scleroderma can live for years, if the illnesses were controlled. She stated that controlling the illnesses would be our first task. So, she started making a list of medicines that would help. She prescribed Imuran, Prednisone, Nifedipine, Cellcept, and aspirin. Each medicine served its own purpose. Furthermore, she wanted me to seek counseling for my depression and come back to her in three weeks to see how I was making out. By then, I would've seen a pulmonologist, rheumatologist, cardiologist, psychologist, and neurologist.

Before I left the office, she asked me if I had any questions. I opened my mouth, but I couldn't speak. She explained to me that it was important for me to stay away from stress, as stress was the number one cause of a flare-up. We both sat there in silence for what seemed like forever.

When she left the room, I sat there crying. I just knew my life was over and that I was going to die. *With two autoimmune illnesses, how could I make it through?* I immediately grew angry. *Why God, why? How could You do this to me? What am I supposed to learn? Nothing!* I began to let my disappointment consume me with anger from that day forward.

Before returning back to the doctor, I had to take a side trip to the hospital. It was my first time in a while, and boy what an experience.. I never had so many needles in my life! My chest hurt so badly. It felt like an elephant was sitting on me eating peanuts, watching the evening news. Every time I inhaled, the pain shattered my back and chest cavities.

After having a CT scan, I was told that I only had forty-five percent usage left of my lungs. The rest had hardened with fibrosis, which meant I had Interstitial Lung Disease, which was something they couldn't fix. They also said I had pneumonia, and that I had given it to myself! I aspirated into my lungs, which meant my digestive system was at risk.

At this point, I had a pulmonologist, rheumatologist, gastroenterologist, pain doctor, and internist at my bedside. It was so overwhelming and I felt all alone. *How would you feel if you were me? What would you say to God? How would you feel about God?*

By this time, news had gotten out that I was chronically ill and my friend circle slowly got smaller and smaller, until no one called me to hang anymore.

Everything happened so fast. My emotions were set on high. My first feeling was emptiness, then abandonment, and then deep depression. Once they all left, I cried. I did a lot of crying; crying was good for me. It wasn't a pity party; it was a good release of stress and anger. I cried about it, wiped the tears off, and shook it off.

This was not an easy process. I didn't fully understand everything until I was far along in my journey of faith, which made all the difference in this race called life! I discovered that you can go through a period of time where everyone you know suddenly knows how to cure what you have. In reality, they may be treating you like a guinea pig, giving you medical advice without even fully understanding what they're suggesting. This is where advocacy comes in.

If all else fails, you have to be your own best advocate. After all, you know your body and what's best for you. Don't allow anyone to treat you the way you don't wish to be treated. Do your homework. Read up on your illness. Read up on your medications and their side effects. And without a doubt, please believe that God is in everything and that He is working it all out for your good!

Praising God during the bad times is just as important as

praising Him throughout the good times. He wants us to thank Him, no matter what our circumstances are. Our human side tends to hide inside instead of reaching out. Praising God is good medicine to the mind, spirit, and body.

> *And the peace of God, which passeth all under-standing, shall keep your hearts and minds through Christ Jesus.*

— Philippians 4:7 KJV

Reflection Questions

1. Has there ever been a time in your life when you doubted God? How can my experience help you turn around your situation?

_____

_____

_____

_____

_____

2. How do you experience God's peace in your life?

_____

_____

_____

_____

_____

3. Who advocates for you? Why?

_____

_____

_____

_____

_____

Prayer for Strength & Healing

I invite you to pray the following prayer with me in faith.

Dear God, shine Your light on whatever is dark in me. Give me strength for the things that seem unbearable. Fix my brokenness. Tend to my bruises. Heal all of the sickness within me. Restore the love, peace, and joy that lives inside of me. In Your most gracious and holy name, Christ Jesus, I pray. Amen.

Let, I pray thee,
thy merciful
kindness be for my
comfort, according
to thy word unto
thy servant.

PSALM 119:76 KJV

10 "Arise, my darling, my beautiful one,
And come along."
17 "The season of our love has come,
Our vines, 'grapevines.'"

Chapter 2 Theme

2 "I am the arose of aSharon,
The alily of the valleys."

2 ""Like a lily among the thorns,
So is amy darling among the amaidens."

3 ""Like an aapple tree among the trees of the forest,
So is my beloved among the ayoung men.
In his shade I took great delight and sat down,
And his afruit was sweet to my ataste.

4 "He has abrought me to aher abanquet hall,
And his abanner over me is love.

5 "aSustain me with araisin cakes,
Refresh me with aapples,
Because I am alovesick.

6 "Let his left hand be under my head
And his aright hand aembrace me.

7 "I aadjure you, O adaughters of Jerusalem,
By the agazelles or by the ahinds of the field,
That you will not aarouse or aawaken my alove
Until she apleases."

Healing Through Love

My first hospitalization was the beginning of many. It started with weekend stays, and then I graduated to a week in the hospital. Nights were the hardest. The echo of the beeping monitors and IV pumps rang out in my head. To have a sense of normalcy, I even tried taking my mind off of my illness. That strategy worked for about three years, but truthfully, I spent more time in the hospital than at work. I thought I was helping my husband and our family life, but that wasn't going so well, either. My health was declining very quickly. My medicine list had increased greatly. I was also taking chemotherapy to try to slow things down. My heart and brain were now affected, and my depression had elevated to a psychiatric level. I hit a real low and unfortunately, it was time to go out on disability.

October 10, 2010 was my last day of work. Although I understood why I needed to leave on disability, I missed the fellowship that came with working in an office environment. So much in my life was changing. My doctors had to put me on more medications now that additional organs were affected. I was already taking twenty-five pills a day!

At home, my behavior changed drastically. I was very unhappy and snappy. I wanted to move out from my mother-in-law's house. I believed that if we were in our own environment as a family, things would be better. And perhaps with the change, my husband wouldn't be so distant.

With everything going on, my husband was overwhelmed with stress. On top of that, it felt as if he didn't care that I was sick. He was never home. I felt alone in my illness, parenting, mind, and marriage. The place where I was heading was too dangerous.

I talked to him about us using my tax refund to move out of his mother's house; he didn't seem to agree. He didn't understand my position and we were at odds. As soon as I got my tax refund, I moved. It didn't matter who disagreed with me because I knew that I needed my own space as a wife and mother. I couldn't live under his mother's roof any longer; I wasn't brought up that way. Three years was more than enough. I had responsibilities and I had to take care of them.

Looking back, I believe that moving out took my marriage to a dark place. And as a result, my depression intensified and I ended up spending many hours weeping in a walk-in closet. At home, my husband didn't feel respected; I walked all over his manhood and took control over our family. My husband slipped further and further away. My kids missed him and didn't really understand what was going on. I spent all my time in my walk-in closet in the dark, crying and hiding from the world. Most of the time, my kids' dinner consisted of canned or fast food. It felt like my life was over. My husband didn't want me and I was getting sicker by the moment. Then, my hair began falling out. Who would want me anyway? I *felt* like nothing. I *had* nothing. I *was* nothing. I just wanted to disappear!

> *God is our refuge and strength, a very present help in trouble.*
>
> — Psalm 46:1 KJV

If my fundamental belief wasn't that this marriage was of God, I would have given up already. Instead, I believed in God for restoration. Just like a house, our body needs a good foundation, as we may experience spiritual warfare on a daily basis. It's important to start your day with God, which will provide you with spiritual strength and support for your life. Before you get out of bed to face the day, it's important to give it to God. The devil wants you to think that calling on God will get you nowhere. Do not let the devil make you question your faith. God knows when you are ready to receive your blessing. God wants you to draw nigh to Him!

God was in the process of bringing our marriage to a place where it could not survive without Him. We were so comfortable doing things separately and without God, that we fell off by the wayside. We were quickly reminded when God put us in a position of needing each other and needing Him. When my health took a turn for the worse and my lungs collapsed, it was then that we realized how foolish we were being. We realized that our marriage and family meant more to us than ever before. It was then that my husband became the man I grew to fall more in love with each passing day. His support and attention were at my beck and call. Going to a doctor's appointment was a new experience for me, but a realization for him. I'm not sure that he realized how serious my illness was until then.

To this day, I truly believe that God pushed us until we fell to our knees. *And guess what?* I'm still there. That's the safest place to be. Don't ever feel condemned because you've cried out to God. He wants you to come to Him and open your heart. He wants a close and personal relationship with you. He wants you to indulge in His love and *become* love.

> *Charity suffereth long, and is kind; charity envieth not; charity vaunteth not itself, is not puffed up, doth not behave itself unseemly, seeketh not her own, is not easily provoked, thinketh no evil; rejoiceth not in iniquity, but rejoiceth in the truth; beareth all things, believeth all things, hopeth all things, endureth all things. Charity never faileth: but whether there be prophecies, they shall fail; whether there be tongues, they shall cease; whether there be knowledge, it shall vanish away.*
>
> — 1 Corinthians 13:4-8 KJV

Upon reading the aforementioned Scripture, the last verse tends to stand out. My husband and I both know it quite well. Although we've been through so much in our eleven years of marriage, love has been the anchor that has stabilized us. We are truly thankful to God for preserving us.

Reflection Questions

1. How has reading this chapter helped you in your current situation?

_____

_____

_____

_____

_____

2. What new revelation has God revealed to you?

_____

_____

_____

_____

_____

3. How does your spiritual strength help others?

_____

_____

_____

_____

_____

4. Has there been a time where your kindness made a huge impact on someone else? *Who* was affected? *Why* was it impactful? *When* did this occur?

_____

_____

_____

_____

_____

Prayer Over Your Day

I invite you to pray the following prayer with me in faith.

> *Heavenly Father, thank You for waking me up today. I pray that my behaviors and actions are pleasing to You. God, You know my struggles and the desires of my heart. So, at this very moment, I give them all to You. My heart and mind will not be troubled because You are in control. You are my spiritual rock that I stand upon. I submit my life to You; my life is in Your hands. You are my Lord and Savior. In Your holy Name, I pray. Amen.*

And God shall wipe
away all tears from their
eyes; and there shall be
no more death, neither
sorrow, nor crying,
neither shall there be
any more pain: for the
former things are
passed away.

REVELATION 21:4 KJV

16 "Our *couch is* luxuriant.
 And the *beams* of
 Indeed, our *couch is* luxuriant.
17 "The *beams* of our *houses are* cedars,
 Our rafters, *cypresses.*

2 "*I am the *rose of *Sharon,
 The *lily of the valleys."

2 "Like a lily among the thorns,
 So is *my darling among the *maidens."

3 "Like an *apple tree among the trees of the forest,
 So is my beloved among the *young men.
 In his shade I took great delight and sat down,
 And his *fruit was sweet to my *taste.
4 "He has *brought me to his *banquet hall,
 And his *banner over me is love.
5 "Sustain me with *raisin cakes,
 Refresh me with *apples,
 Because I am *lovesick.
6 "Let his left hand be under my head,
 And his right hand embrace me.

7 "*Swear to me, O daughters of *Jerusalem,
 By the *gazelles or by the *hinds of the field,
 That you *do not arouse or awaken *my love
 Until she pleases."

Healing Through Grace

Blaming yourself for other people's actions and behaviors is the worst thing you can do, especially when you have a chronic illness. It can cause additional pressure on top of your depressed state. I blamed myself for what happened between my husband and I. I felt like things were my fault. Looking back, I can honestly say that it wasn't all his or my fault.

Change means growth. However, not everyone grows or changes at the same pace. Some may stay stagnant, no matter how much you minister to them; if they have a reluctant spirit, they won't change. However, there are others who may flourish because they are open to change.

Change requires letting go of self-sabotaging thoughts and embracing God's freedom for our lives. So often, we can be our own worst enemy and block ourselves from receiving the rewards God has for us.

For sin shall not have dominion over you: for ye are
not under the law, but under grace.

— Romans 6:14 KJV

I spent many nights alone, trying to figure out where I went wrong and why this was happening to our marriage. My depression was at its lowest. My husband used work, hobbies, and anything else as an excuse to not come home on time. My insecure mind began to wonder about infidelity. *Could I blame him?* I was sick and felt like I was dying, little by little. *Who would want me?* Those thoughts continued to haunt me. As time passed, my thoughts proved to be true and things were revealed to me. His late night endeavors involved the company of someone else.

The day that I realized what was going on, my world came crashing in; I felt like I died inside. I was a good wife. I didn't deserve this; our kids didn't deserve this. I immediately became sick to my stomach at the thought of him being with another woman. Death seemed to be the only way out of my own suffocation; I sunk into a deep depression. I sent my sons away to a sitter every chance I could, just to be alone in my pain. When I couldn't send them off, I would go to my walk-in closet and spend a lot of time in there crying out to God. I didn't understand the path my life had taken.

Each time I talked to my husband about the situation, it ended up in an argument. He couldn't explain why things happened the way they did. I needed to know why so that I could fix things because that is what I am— a fixer. I wanted to fix our marriage, but I couldn't do it alone.

One weekend when I sent the kids away, my depression was so intense that I tried to take my life. Everything I was facing rose to the surface— having an illness, raising the kids alone, having a loveless marriage, accepting my husband's infidelity, and having a surplus of bills. I didn't know which end was up!

While crying, I made a phone call to my cousin, who was a rock and good advisor in my life. I cried about what was going on and she consoled me; she told me some things I needed to hear and didn't want to hear. She was always very honest with me. I was so hurt and in pain. My heart was so broken that my body ached. She expressed her fear regarding what I may do. So, she informed me that she would be on the next flight from Bermuda to come see me. My brother also knew what happened; he and I were also very close. Therefore, he also decided to take the next flight from Bermuda to be with me. Both my cousin and brother wanted to come for support and ensure that I didn't do anything drastic.

After the call, I crawled into bed and decided that my life wasn't worth living anymore. I felt worthless. *Who would want me?* I was a sick mother on oxygen, that was bitter and scorned. After all, my own husband didn't want me. So, I took a bunch of pills and cried myself off to sleep.

The next day, I woke up with such a big headache. It was obvious that God had other plans for me because I was still here— alive and kicking! However, the cavalry flown in to ridicule me for what I tried to do, and my headache grew worse. My brother and cousin arrived; in short, they told me off. They asked me what I was thinking! They assured me that I'm worthy, have so much promise, and that I am one of God's precious gifts. From that day forward, I thought of myself as the daughter of the Most High God, who sacrificed His life to save mine. How awesome is that?! They both stayed through the weekend to love on me and assure me that things will be okay.

By the time my boys came back, I tried to have a new outlook on life. My goal was to be more attentive and only go into my closet when I was looking for clothes— no more crying, no more hiding! It was time to come out the closet and into the world.

Reflection Questions

1. Has there ever been a time when you felt pushed into a corner, thinking that death was the only way out? Who or what saved your life?

_____

_____

_____

_____

_____

2. How has reading about my turnaround helped you in your current situation??

_____

_____

_____

_____

_____

3. How has the sacrificed Blood of Jesus Christ impacted your life?

_____

_____

_____

_____

_____

Prayer of Cancellation

I invite you to pray the following prayer with me in faith.

Heavenly Father, I ask You to forgive me for my sins and cleanse me from any area where I have allowed the enemy to enter. I declare and decree that all negative word curses spoken over me must die in the Name of Jesus. I thank You that those curses will no longer operate against me. I bind the spirit of depression, suicide, and mental illness of all kinds in the Name of Jesus Christ. Amen.

Neither be ye
sorry, for the joy
of the Lord is your
strength.

NEHEMIAH 8:10B KJV

Chapter 2 Theme

2 "I am the rose of Sharon,
The lily of the valleys."

2 "Like a lily among the thorns,
So is my darling among the maidens."

3 "Like an apple tree among the trees of the forest,
So is my beloved among the young men.
In his shade I took great delight and sat down,
And his fruit was sweet to my taste.

4 "He has brought me to his banquet hall,
And his banner over me is love.

5 "Sustain me with raisin cakes,
Refresh me with apples,

Healing Through Guidance

It took several months for me to pull myself together. I had to keep leaning on God's guidance to get through it all. It was coming to the end of my lease, and for the upcoming year, they were raising my rent another $150.00. Because I couldn't afford it, I had to think about where to go and what to do. Going backward was not an option, so I pulled all my resources together and a good friend offered for us to stay with her in Delaware. My husband did not seem to care, as he offered nothing, and had no issue with us leaving. So, I put everything in storage, and off we went.

While driving to Delaware, my eyes burned with tears. My heart was broken and my mind was confused. *Was this the end of my marriage? Did I just walk out on what I thought was love?* I know for sure that I loved him, but being in love is a different thing. Every time I looked at my husband, the pain resurfaced. The enemy would toy with my emotions and I would have thoughts of him with someone else. As a result, moving away seemed to be better and better by the moment.

My initial plan was to only spend the summer in Delaware. I planned to use that time to find another affordable apartment in Maryland; however, things didn't go as planned. As time drew closer for the kids to go to school, I began to panic because I couldn't find a place for us to live. As the days passed and school drew near, I widened my search, only to come up with nothing. Financially, I just couldn't afford it without my husband.

About one week before school started for the boys, I found an apartment just outside of Delaware. However, I needed my husband to make it work. It was hard calling him for that reason. We hadn't spoken much over the summer, although he did visit several times to see the kids. Within one week, he made sure we had the apartment, retrieved all of our things from storage, and were safely into the new place. I registered the boys in the nearest schools for the 2011-2012 school year and exhaled. Elkton, here we come!

Living in Elkton, MD wasn't that bad. My husband commuted to work in Washington, D.C., which was about an hour to work and an hour back. Some nights, he stayed at his mother's if he worked late. But most of the time, he was home with us. Things seemed to be going well for us all. Now, we were living right and doing things in line with God's will. God was our number one focus. We stayed prayed up and read our Bibles regularly.

We attended church in Newark, Delaware. It was a marvelous church with wonderful, lovable people. The pastor was a good teacher and preacher of the Word Of God. They welcomed us in and loved us right from the beginning. We never felt like strangers; we always felt like family. My health was steady, my husband was happy, and the kids were doing well. About a year later, however, things changed.

In 2012, my health took a decline; it all started with inconti-nence. One day, while we were in the store, I suddenly smelled something not too nice! Little did I know, it was me! I had pooped on myself, unknowingly. So, I respectfully put my cart to the side, found my husband and kids, and quietly told my husband what happened. Then, we quickly left and went straight home. He helped me get out of my nasty clothes, put them in the trash, and stepped away for me to bathe. While bathing, I sank in the water, pouring my heart out to God. "Please, oh God! Heal me," I pleaded. However, that was only the beginning.

Leading up to Christmas 2012, my health began to decline rapidly. My digestive system broke down; I couldn't swallow and my food would not properly digest. Soon afterward, my lungs collapsed. This time, I was in really bad shape and had an extended stay in the hospital.

I was in the hospital for what seemed like forever. It was so bad that when they discharged me, I had to go to a rehabilita-tion center to stay until I was ready to go home. While I was there, I found out that my husband didn't pay any rent for two months and that we were being evicted. I couldn't believe my ears! This was around Christmas— the worst time to be evicted! *Why didn't he talk to me about it?* All this time, we could have gotten financial assistance. His response was that the finances got away from him and that he couldn't keep up. This was when we hit rock bottom.

I was released from the rehabilitation center a few days earlier, so I could pack up my house before December 31. Despite being taped up and in stitches, I did what I had to do. Members from our church helped us pack up the house in one night! Everything except our clothing was put in a storage container. My husband left, saying he would see us soon. The boys and I went to live in a shelter. Looking back, I believe this was the wrong move by both of us. He left and I let him leave, knowing the situation. At that point, I could have fought harder for my marriage. However, because I felt like he didn't, why should I?

Despite how I felt, I knew what God desired. God wants us to bring our problems to Him and lay them at His feet. They are His battles, not ours. The minute you take control, things get out of control.

> *Though I walk in the midst of trouble, thou wilt revive me: thou shalt stretch forth thine hand against the wrath of mine enemies, and thy right hand shall save me. The Lord will perfect that which concerneth me: thy mercy, O Lord, endureth for ever: forsake not the works of thine own hands.*
>
> — Psalm 138:7-8 KJV

After about two months at the shelter, I realized it was a cult! Therefore, I packed up my kids and we literally ran for our lives! We ended up at a sleazy motel. It was all I could afford, and my children needed me to be strong, no matter what my health looked like. This was the beginning of the end of my marriage.

While staying at the hotel, some of our church family brought us groceries and dinner. Thankfully, this was during the summer, so it didn't interfere with the kids' schooling. Living like this was very difficult with two children under the age of ten. My husband helped us out as much as he could, but it was not enough. It was just enough to pay the hotel bill.

After a few weeks of living like this, my health began to decline. I had to have emergency surgery! Because of everything going on, my husband and I decided to separate the kids, so that it would be easier. Everyone we reached out to for support had to work, and my husband's schedule was not flexible enough to help Josiah, as much as he needed. So, Josiah went to stay with his godmother, while Ellijah went to his sister's house in Baltimore.

> *For I know the thoughts that I think toward you,*
>   *saith the Lord, thoughts of peace, and not of*
>   *evil, to give you an expected end.*
>
> — Jeremiah 29:11 KJV

Now that the boys were in good care, I was able to focus on my health. When I went to the doctor, they ran a series of digestive tests. I was told that my digestive system had been failing and that I needed surgery. My esophagus was broken and I could only digest with the help of gravity. My sphincter muscle was stuck open. That was so painful. As a result, the doctor wanted to do a surgery called Nissen Fundoplication to address my condition. It was a very difficult procedure that would keep me in the hospital for about two weeks. And afterwards, I would need to rest at home for a while. I agreed to this arrangement because the pain was so severe; I threw up almost every day after eating.

On the day of the surgery, the doctor assured me that all would be well. So, off to sleep I went! When I woke up, the pain was deadly. The surgery incision was up and down my entire stomach. I was stapled all the way up. It was excruciatingly painful. I was having trouble eating, so they had to give me a feeding tube. That was not fun at all! To this day, I still have a hole in my stomach. Having an autoimmune illness makes it harder for your body to heal. Because of that, I thought I would never heal. However, I was in it for the long haul. I trusted God for my complete healing.

Reflection Questions

1. Is there a time in your life when you truly had to rely on God?

_____

_____

_____

_____

_____

2. How has reading this chapter helped you in your current situation?

_____

_____

_____

_____

_____

3. After reading Jeremiah 29:11, what are your thoughts about your current situation?

_____

_____

_____

_____

_____

Prayer for Strength

I invite you to pray the following prayer with me in faith.

Heavenly Father, I thank You for Your guidance. Thank You for Your mercy. Please give me the strength to endure this situation and help me find the blessing in the things I do not understand. Lord, You know every decision I have to make and every challenge that I face. Forgive me, Lord, for trying to do life on my own without your guidance and wisdom. I need you, Lord. In Your glorious and merciful name, I pray. Amen.

Heal me, O Lord, and
I shall be healed;
save me, and I shall
be saved: for thou
art my praise.

JEREMIAH 17:14 KJV

Chapter 2 Theme

2 "I am the ²rose of Sharon,
The ³lily of the valleys."

2 "¹Like a lily among the thorns,
So is ²my darling among the ³maidens."

3 "¹Like an ²apple tree among the trees of the forest,
So is my beloved among the ³young men.
In his shade I took great delight and sat down,
And his ⁴fruit was sweet to my ⁵taste.

4 "He has ¹brought me to his ²banquet hall,
And his ³banner over me is love.

Healing Through Change

After my surgery, I recuperated at my best friend's house. Over a period of twenty-one years, our friendship went through many ups and downs. We were so close that it was hard to deny. We shared many good times and bad times, together. This was true friendship.

Our jokes and tears go back to 2000. One funny moment, in particular, occurred one day when we were starving and went to get chicken from Popeyes. She was so hungry and quickly started to eat, not realizing that she would bite her finger after sticking the chicken in her mouth! This memory brings me constant laughter; it's truly one that I will never forget.

Because of our closeness, living my friend while I recuperated was easy, to say the least. While I was there, I had a wound vac nurse come to her house to care for me. She cleaned and wrapped my wound three times a week. This process went on for about two months.

In early September, I went to a shelter called Sarah's House. I wanted to have both of my boys with me and my friend's house would have been too small for all three of us. I also knew that Sarah's House would help me get on my feet and get my own place, although moving there was a great sacrifice. Ellijah decided that he wanted to stay with his sister. He didn't want to be in a shelter again, and I didn't blame or force him.

Living in a shelter was a rude awakening. Having someone dictate what you can and can't do, tell you what to do, and control when you can come and go was hard. Josiah had a hard time adapting, as well. He went through a really bad cycle of hitting and biting me while there. One of the rules was that you cannot physically discipline your child, and he knew it. It was really tough for me and emotionally draining. Staying there for four to six months was my mission and I stuck to that. I was determined, strong, and resilient. I had faith that I could save money and make it out. While I was there, I found out that there were many people who were repeat offenders— those who have been there more than once because they couldn't survive life on the outside. However, I knew that would never be me.

March arrived, and I was ready to leave. I saved all of my child support payments and moved into our own apartment. We were in the same complex as my best friend. I wanted to be near her so we could help each other. Not having Ellijah with me during that time played on my mind and my heart. I felt like I just gave him away. I hardly saw him and it hurt, tremen-dously. Since it hurt me, I wondered if it hurt him, too.

Having my own place finally brought both of my boys together with me, which was a blessing. But at times, it still felt empty. I was barely getting used to not having my husband and sleeping alone. Some nights were better than others. My husband would come by and get the boys to spend time with him on the weekends, but I was never included. I could feel him slipping away. We didn't really have much to say to each other, except that it was time for a divorce.

After two years of separation and many arguments, I filed for a divorce. It hurt so badly. It felt like I was suffering from a broken heart. So, I thought that it was the perfect time for me to begin a medication regimen and to develop a stronger spiritual focus in my life. During this time, I was looking for a church family. I missed fellowship and longed to be in the house of the Lord.

While riding in an Uber one day, I met a guy named Chris; he told me all about the church he attended. He even said that he would pick me up if I didn't have a ride. So, when Sunday came, I went.

Attending this new church was such an experience! At first, I went through many emotions, until I experienced the real gift, which was the Holy Spirit. The love that I experienced from the members was so beautiful. Although I was closed off and a little reluctant to make friends at first, it was still a very comfortable atmosphere. I love the fact that it was a teaching church and a loving environment.

After service, the pastors met with the visitors; we had snacks and were able to talk with them. They were so real and transparent. The pastors poured out so much that it caused me to meditate on what was preached. Meditation is good for the heart, mind, and body. However you feel comfortable— with or without music— it's important to meditate on God's Word. Meditation helps relieve stress and promotes resilience. It's a great opportunity to soak in praise and worship music, settle your spirit and soul, and bask in His presence. Meditation enabled me to release everything I was going through with my health and relationship to God, and wait patiently to hear from Him.

Going through a divorce with children is challenging. Although it was hard, I committed to attending mediation to help us work through this new process of change. Sharing secrets and intimate moments of your marriage to a complete stranger in mediation was uncomfortable, to say the least. My husband admitted to his indiscretion and openly apologized for hurting me. After the meeting, we went and had lunch together to discuss our parenting relationship. It was a good lunch and great decisions were made.

Divorce can be hard on children, if you're not careful. Ellijah was fine. He was older and understood more. Josiah, on the other hand, took it rather hard. He had an intense breakdown and I signed him up for counseling. He really wanted us back together. However, I understood that his healing would take time. I assured him that I would always be there to pick up the pieces. One thing I knew for sure was that our boys loved us dearly. And to me, that's all that mattered.

Once things were settled down and final, we were officially divorced. My ex-husband and I learned to communicate well to ensure that our co-parenting was healthy. Our boys were able to adjust and things were going really well for a while— until my health started acting up again.

It started out as a throbbing pain, on the side under my rib. I was rushed to the hospital once again, only to find out that I was having complications with my gallbladder. I needed to have surgery, yet again. What made matters even worse was that the staff at the hospital actually knew me by name, because I was always there. What may seem to be routine to a typical hospital patient may not be the same to a lupus patient. People with lupus have complex systems; our medical check list is lengthy. Healing often takes longer. And for those of us who have lung issues, breathing becomes an issue. As a result, doctors are often concerned with intubation and how they can perform surgery without aggravating any previous symptoms. This makes the overall process complicated. But at times, it's easier to deal with. However, I usually end up having to embrace the challenge head on.

Reflection Questions

1. What is your takeaway from this chapter?

_____

_____

_____

_____

_____

2. How do your friends view you? Do you wear your illness?

_____

_____

_____

_____

_____

3. Do you dress for the job you want or the job you have?

_____

_____

_____

_____

_____

4. Do you have an advocate? Who are they and why do you have them?

_____

_____

_____

_____

_____

Prayer of Thanking God

I invite you to pray the following prayer with me in faith.

Dear God thank you for my life. Thank you for what you have done for me and my family. You have done so much more than I could ever have imagined. You comfort me, provide for me, and love me. You have shown your unconditional love by being there for me and with me everyday. Thank you Lord for never leaving me Amen.

Notwithstanding
the Lord stood
with me, and
strengthened me.

2 TIMOTHY 4:17A KJV

Chapter 2 Theme

2 "I am the rose of Sharon,
The lily of the valleys."

2 "Like a lily among the thorns,
So is my darling among the maidens."

3 "Like an apple tree among the trees of the forest,
So is my beloved among the young men.
In his shade I took great delight and sat down,
And his fruit was sweet to my taste.

4 "He has brought me to his banquet hall,
And his banner over me is love.

5 "Sustain me with raisin cakes,
Refresh me with apples,
Because I am lovesick.

Healing Through Relationship

My prayer life had become so rich. I continued attending the church I visited, and officially joined. They were young pastors and radicals for Jesus Christ; they truly had the glory of the Lord on them! Being around them is so intoxicating; it compels you to want to glean from them. I really enjoyed the teaching component and the praise and worship music. Life at my new church was truly amazing.

About two months later, things took a turn for the worst. On June 26, 2016, I was scared to death. In the middle of the night, Ellijah was on a bicycle in the street with a friend, and got struck head on by a car. They were not supposed to be out this time of night. When the police arrived to my door, they had snide remarks and assured me that it was only a broken leg. He also added on some parenting tips, but I was too concerned for my child to listen to that.

Calling Baltimore Shock Trauma took a lot of strength; my stomach was in knots. After I was informed of the date and time of the procedure, I hung up and cried. It really hit me hard. Next, I had to call his dad! *How do I tell him this?* That was one of the hardest things I've ever had to tell him. To my surprise, he was much calmer than me. I cried and cried. Once he calmed me down, I hung up and fell to my knees in prayer, which is where I should have been all along.

Behold, God is my salvation; I will trust, and not be afraid: for the Lord Jehovah is my strength and my song; he also is become my salvation.

— Isaiah 12:2 KJV

Six o'clock in the morning hit hard. I sprung to my feet already dressed, waiting for my ex-husband to pick me up, so we could go to the hospital together. When I first saw my son, I died a thousand deaths. His body was mangled. He already had emergency surgery on both legs and his left thumb. His neck was in a brace due to spinal damage; his face was fractured. I knew from that day forward, on June 27, 2016, that I wasn't leaving the hospital, and I didn't.

Ellijah was bedridden for four months. I had to help him bathe, brush his teeth, and have a sense of normalcy each day. While I was in the hospital with Ellijah, Josiah stayed with his dad and visited on the weekends, only. When my ex-husband came on Tuesdays, Thursdays, and Saturdays he brought clean clothes for me.

Once Ellijah was released, his recovery was slow. He had to do a series of physical therapy exercises, which left him in pain. I reminded him of what he survived and that he could do it. To this day, he still has some challenges, but it never stops him from being all he can be.

God is our refuge and strength, a very present help
in trouble.

— Psalm 46:1 KJV

Shortly afterwards, we received a notice to move; it was done amicably. They felt it was too much loitering in the area; Ellijah was identified as one of the loiterers. They assured me that this was not an eviction. The simply wanted me to move quietly. I agreed, as the loitering was too much for me, also.

We packed up our belongings and moved to another home, just in time for Christmas. Although Josiah had to change schools, it was an opportunity for him to make new friends. However, Josiah found it hard to make new friends, but not Ellijah. He quickly made new friends and had many of them!

Life in our new environment was okay, until it rained. For some reason, whenever it rained outside, the carpet would get wet. I called maintenance several times, but one could explain it. When the ceiling fell in, that was the horse that broke the camel's back. The ceiling that fell was soaked in urine and had feces stains. So, they had to clean everything up and replace it. After enduring these horrible living conditions for two years, it was time to go. However, while I was there, I developed a new friendship with a woman who also attended my new church. It was great having our children connected. Our friendship grew to be so close. Over time, I learned that she's a great teacher of the Word of God and is a true confidant. She was truly someone I could laugh and cry with. She is someone near and dear to my heart. I thank God for her. To this day, she teaches me so many things about God and life, as she is well-versed in both areas.

Thou art my hiding place; thou shalt preserve me

from trouble; thou shalt compass me about with
songs of deliverance. Selah. I will instruct thee
and teach thee in the way which thou shalt go: I
will guide thee with mine eye.

— Psalm 32:7-8 KJV

After the ceiling disaster, we finally moved to our new home. It wasn't a bad place, although there were some issues. The house was full of roaches. No matter how many times we called for extermination, they always came back. I think they liked the roach spray and it made them multiply. Also, it was not the safest area. The police frequented the area due to gunshots and loitering. Something always happened at the bottom of the hill. The kids couldn't play outside. It just wasn't safe.

While in this new environment, I met another woman who I can truly call my friend. She was my neighbor for two years and had sons, just like me. Being friends with her showed me that there are truly kind people in this world. She was an absolute stranger who opened up her home and her heart. Throughout the time we were neighbors, she watched out for my youngest son while I was sick. She ensured that he was never left alone. She took him in as though he was hers and never had an agenda. To this day, our boys are good friends and our friendship is stronger than ever! It is truly a blessing to have strong, healthy relationships.

As my relationships with others flourished, so did my relationship with Christ. My prayer life became stronger as I read the Word of God and joined the supernatural school at my church. I learned the true importance of studying the Word and how it enhances your life by nourishing your body and soul.

This was so important to me, as I needed so much healing physically, emotionally, mentally, and spiritually. Just by attending school, I opened up my heart more. I truly believed God for my healing— so much so, that I began to walk in that manifestation. I even joined the worship team and began to sing for the Lord! It was the most exhilarating and glorious feeling I've ever experienced! I've sang in choirs before, but this feeling was new. God was singing through me to the saints. This was a beautiful experience! I could feel their love for Christ Jesus and rejoiced with them through song. It was the most amazing and humbling experience. It's so wonderful how God can change your life in an instant. When you align your faith with His promises, you can experience His grace upon your life.

Reflection Questions

1. What are you thankful for? Why?

_____

_____

_____

_____

_____

2. What does Psalm 46:1 mean to you?

_____

_____

_____

_____

_____

3. What is your takeaway from this chapter? How can this knowledge help enrichen your life?

_____

_____

_____

_____

_____

Prayer of Thankfulness

I invite you to pray the following prayer with me in faith.

Father God, thank You for waking me up today. To have another day to worship Your Name and sing Your praises gives my heart joy. Continue to let Your light shine through me, each and every day. Make me more like You, Lord, so that I may treasure my blessings, no matter how small. In Your most gracious name, I pray. Amen.

For the eyes of the Lord are over the righteous, and his ears are open unto their prayers.

1 PETER 3:12A KJV

Chapter 2 Theme

2 "I am the *rose of *Sharon,
The *lily of the valleys."

2 "Like a lily among the thorns,
So is *my darling among the *maidens."

3 "Like an *apple tree among the trees of the forest,
So is my beloved among the *young men.
In his shade I took great delight and sat down,
And his *fruit was sweet to my *taste.
4 "He has *brought me to his *banquet hall,
And his *banner over me is love.
5 *Sustain me with *raisin cakes,
Refresh me with *apples,
Because I am *lovesick.

Healing Through Gratitude

Over the past two years, my health was very poor. It was so bad that I needed an in-home nurse. She was an absolute blessing! This occurred at the same time as the COVID-19 pandemic, a deadly virus that rocked and paralyzed the world. To say that many died is an understatement. From every corner of the world, the pandemic left its wrath. In the United States, one of the hardest places hit was New York City. No matter how bad the condition of the world was, my nurse still came each day to care for me. Even when the government shut everything down, she was considered an essential worker and went above and beyond to ensure my safety.

During this time, my church family was beyond wonderful. They prayed for my family, continuously. My pastors have been such an example of God's love for me. They have shown me true friendship, leadership, and love. They made sure that there was always food in my fridge or on the table. They readily provided support and counseling. It's the first church I've stayed at for so long and experienced such love. The outpouring of love from the congregation is amazing, as well. If ever I doubted the love from my church family, I have no reason to doubt now. I have to say, it's been so many wonderful years, and I look forward to the years to come.

In December 2020, we officially moved to Belmawr. And of course, when moving day comes, there's always a hiccup. But God already sent his angels out as a hedge of protection. I received a tremendous blessing that day from someone who simply showed up. She may not have known the impact of her presence, but I am truly grateful for the support that I received that day. She was like an angel in human form— genuine, honest, and trustworthy.

And now the Lord shew kindness and truth unto
you: and I also will requite you this kindness,
because ye have done this thing.

— 2 Samuel 2:6 KJV

Moving into my new house was exciting. It was set up like a small townhome. I absolutely loved it! It was by far one of the nicest places we've lived. There were no roaches; it was very clean and extremely quiet. However, things came to a screeching halt when I contracted the COVID-19 virus.

On January 1, 2021, I was hospitalized at a local hospital. I was fighting a fever, chills, cough, and breathing issues. My family was extremely concerned because of my health challenges, I was already a high-risk person and some might say that I was marked for death. I received a COVID-19 test and it came back positive. Afterward, I was immediately admitted. I cried. I was alone and afraid. They quickly medicated me and got me as settled as possible. After a vigorous six days of medical treatment and attention, the doctors thought that I was well enough to go home.

On January 7th, I went home. However, things weren't getting any better; they only got worse. My pastors and church family consistently prayed for me. On January 10th, my fever spiked and my breathing was sporadic. I could hardly talk. While on the phone with my pastors, they suggested calling the ambulance. When I got to the hospital, they did their normal blood work and said that I was okay. Although they said that my blood work was fine, but my body said something else. They didn't listen to what I said and released me.

On January 12th, I was taken back to the hospital by a church member who dropped me off. My symptoms were even worse. My breathing was so bad that I couldn't even speak to tell them what was wrong with me. My pulse-ox reading was 87%. It was supposed to be between 95-100%. So, they admitted me and rushed me back to the hospital bed, only to realize that I was recently there for the same thing— but now, the symptoms were worse. So, the hospital staff quickly jumped into action. When they discovered that my doctors were at Hopkins, I was quickly transferred there. My pastors sent out church-wide prayers for me. I could feel the prayers. I could feel the love being poured out over me like water drenching my body. I had never felt such love from a church before. They called regularly to find out my prognosis.

Once I was settled at Hopkins, the doctors informed me that I had fungal pneumonia in my lungs. It was pretty bad. I could hardly breathe to talk. Nights were the hardest. I cried myself to sleep, as I was not getting better fast enough. I wasn't letting God work on me and in me. I was so afraid that I let it cloud my judgement. Instead of using my time to read the Word or worship, I just laid there, almost giving up.

One day, I talked to my pastor and he said, "Are you scared?" I replied, "Yes. Yes, I am." He comforted me and let me know that it's okay to be scared. It's a scary situation. He reminded me how strong I was and all that I had overcome in the past. He stated that he was proud of me. Not many have said that to me in my life. From that point on, I prayed for strength to overcome this situation. I prayed for my health to be restored better than it was. Nights were easy after that.

Gradually my health started to turn around for the best. After fourteen days, I was able to come home to my boys. To this day, I regularly meet with the infectious disease doctors and am still on antifungal medicine to maintain healthy blood levels.

While lying on my stomach, I had incredible pain in my lower abdomen, only to discover a tennis ball-sized lump. Upon the doctors examining me, it was definitively stated that it was not a hernia, and that a CT scan was needed to further diagnose the problem.

Be not wise in thine own eyes: fear the Lord, and
depart from evil. It shall be health to thy navel,
and marrow to thy bones.

— Proverbs 3:7-8 KJV

After a week of waiting, I went in for the CT scan. Trying to get an IV in my arm was very difficult, which is why I had to get a chest port. After being stuck numerous times, they finally got a vein and the IV contrast was a go. After the procedure, I felt sick to my stomach. Knowing the reason for the scan was enough to make me sick. My mind ran away with thoughts of everything it could be. Also, the hand that they used to insert the IV was swollen and on fire! The tech noticed it first; she was more concerned than me. They gave me a lot of cold water to drink to cool me down, and had me seen by the doctor. As I thought, there was no cause for alarm. However, because they wanted to take precaution, they sent me home with a small care bag, just in case.

While home, the waiting game began. Those next few weeks were especially hard for me. Waiting for the results to come in was not easy. Although I received a preliminary result, it had to be verified by the doctor. So, because it was not clear what it was, I remained calm and steadfast in my prayer for healing. My church family prayed with me.

> *Why art thou cast down, O my soul? And why art*
> *thou disquieted in me? Hope thou in God: for I*
> *shall yet praise him for the help of his counte-*
> *nance. Why art thou cast down, O my soul? And*
> *why art thou disquieted within me? Hope thou*
> *in God: for I shall yet praise him, who is the*
> *health of my countenance, and my God.*
>
> — Psalm 42:5, 11 KJV

My doctor's appointment went well. My overall health seemed to be improving. The lump in question was still a puzzle. The doctor said she wanted to get a second scan and a second opinion from their radiologist to make sure she was covering all bases. Inside, I believe that God healed me, just like He has healed my lungs!

Two weeks later, my doctor called me with the radiologist's

report. I was informed that there was no lump in my stomach. There was nothing to question, at all! God did it again. He is the Great Physician. Hallelujah!

During my Christian walk, my illness has given me much to be thankful for. No one ever thinks that an illness can have that type of impact on you, but it reminds me to count my blessings every day, and to appreciate those who God has blessed me with. Having a chronic illness causes you to stop and reexamine who you are, what's important, and how you define yourself. You have to claim your self-worth and own who you are. Don't give in to the illness and let it control you, control the illness. Lupus has brought me out of my shell and helped me to be a blessing to others in and out of church. I stopped hiding and began to show up to events and embrace who I am, despite this illness. People began to take notice of me, and realized that I had so much to give. I have truly blossomed and have so much to offer. I am special in my own right. God has blessed me with an amazing testimony of His grace. And for that, I am grateful.

Reflection Questions

1. How has reading this chapter influenced the thoughts you have about your overall health and well-being?

_____

_____

_____

_____

_____

2. How has having an illness (in the past or present) caused you to slow down and examine yourself?

_____

_____

_____

_____

_____

3. Do you find that focus groups are helpful? If so, in what way?

_____

_____

_____

_____

_____

4. What are you willing to let go of in order to let God step in?

_____

_____

_____

_____

_____

Prayer of Comfort Through Sickness

I invite you to pray the following prayer with me in faith.

Gracious God, I pray that You will comfort me in my time of suffering. Please give me healing hands to lay on myself and bless my body for the benefit of my cure. Shower me with confidence and the power of Your grace, so that even when I am afraid, I may put my all my trust in You. In Jesus Name, I pray. Amen.

My son, attend to my words; incline thine ear unto my sayings. Let them not depart from thine eyes; keep them in the midst of thine heart. For they are life unto those that find them, and health to all their flesh.

PROVERBS 4:20-22 KJV

2 "I am the ²rose of ⁰Sharon,
The ²lily of the valleys."

2 "²Like a lily among the thorns,
So is ²my darling among the ²maidens."

3 "²Like an ²apple tree among the trees of the forest,
So is my beloved among the ²young men.
In his shade I took great delight and sat down,
And his ²fruit was ²sweet to my ²taste.

4 "He has ²brought me to ²his ²banquet hall,
And his ²banner over me is love.

5 Sustain me with ²raisin cakes,
Refresh me with ²apples,
Because I am ²lovesick.

6 Let his left hand be ²under my head
And his right hand ²embrace me.

7 I ²adjure you, O daughters of Jerusalem,
By the ²gazelles or by the ²hinds of the field,
That you ²do not arouse or awaken my love
Until she ²pleases."

Healing Through Identity

Let's fast forward to 2022! Currently, things are going great! I was blessed with a new house in the new year! It's such a wonderful feeling to have a new, permanent home. We now live in a brand new three-bedroom, two-and-a-half bath townhome. Wow— what a year, so far! You may be wondering: *how did we get here?* Allow me to explain.

Last year, it started with me getting COVID-19 in January, which left me hospitalized for three months. Then, in April I had a stroke. By this time, I was treated like an experiment. The doctors didn't know what to do with me. After they figured things out and got me to a stable position, I spent two weeks in rehab, strengthening my left side. This was totally exciting, to say the least! As June quickly approached, I started to experience a sense of normalcy. Shortly afterwards, my mom transitioned. As much as I wanted to be with my family during this time, I wasn't allowed to travel because I recently had a stroke. The doctors didn't think it was a good idea. When July rolled around, my phone rang. This was a call that I would never forget! Apparently, I was still listed in a housing program that I signed up for when my son was eight years old. At the time of the call, he was twenty-one years old. I was so surprised when I received the call. I was told that I was next in line to receive a brand new home, if I wanted it. *Trick question, right? Who wouldn't want a brand new house?* So, of course I said yes. The lady on the phone informed me that things were almost done and that she would forward me the necessary paperwork. Five months later, we moved into our new home! I absolutely love it here! God truly blessed us!

Regarding my health status, there are still major challenges that I face. My pulmonologist gave me bad news about my lungs. He sent my file to the transplant team who denied me, because some of my health issues made me a bad candidate. Regardless of what they said, I didn't get upset. I'm a firm believer that I am healed and that God is the Great Physician. He knows all things, sees all things, and does all things.

For a while, I had to wear my oxygen mask to church and carry it everywhere I went. I was a bit sad and a little angry because of it. I missed singing worship! It's an unexplainable feeling to be able to worship God Almighty, the King of Kings and Lord of Lords! I missed being able to pour out and minister beautiful words of love, courage, faith, and healing to others. Doing so was truly healing to my soul, as well. So, I made up my mind that I was not going to sit on the bench any longer. So, sure enough, I took off my oxygen mask and began to sing worship again. It was so powerful and healing for me. I learned that despite all that I go through, God is still faithful and has shown me great mercy. Therefore, I wake up each day and give Him honor and praise, for His mercy endures forever.

Regarding my spiritual life, I am stronger than ever. This year was my third and final year of attending the supernatural school at my church. I recently graduated as a licensed minister and it was so fulfilling. While attending Revival Harvest Supernatural School, I learned so much about who I am in Christ, His promises, and His love. I learned how to teach others about God's love, how to be ready in and out of season, how to pray, and how to lead others. I've learned so much! But most of all, I learned that I have a family of people that love me, unconditionally. They have interceded for me, prayed for and with me, cooked for me, picked me up, and called to check in on me. I learned that I have *love*. God's love for me affirms my value, worth, and identity. I know who I am and I can stand proudly on that premise!

Regarding the relationship with my ex-husband, we have become much closer. He has grown considerably and our communication is in a very good place. I have grown to respect him and value his thoughts and opinions more than before. We are thankful to God for preserving our friendship, parenthood, and the genuine love that feel for each other. We nurture it by the love of God and the love that we have for each other to be who we are, authentically. There's absolutely nothing like being who God has called you to be, unashamedly.

Reflection Questions

1. What are you willing to sacrifice to achieve your dreams?

_____

_____

_____

_____

_____

2. What is your heart revealing to you?

_____

_____

_____

_____

_____

3. Are you comfortable in your own skin? Have you accepted who God has called you to be?

_____

_____

_____

_____

_____

Prayer of an Overcomer

I invite you to pray the following prayer with me in faith.

Father, I come before Your throne of grace. Your Word says that I am an overcomer because of the Blood of the Lamb. There is nothing that can defeat You and every victory is mine because of You. I am thankful that I belong to You. You continuously surround me with Your presence and Your love. Thank You for protecting me, so that the enemy cannot touch me. Because you walk with me, I am safe. Your Word in Isaiah 41:12 says, "Fear not, for I am with you; be not dismayed, for I am your God; I will strengthen you, I will help you, I will uphold you with my righteous right hand." Father, I thank You for Your never ending grace. In Jesus Name, I pray. Amen.

Peace I leave with you, my peace I give unto you: not as the world giveth, give I unto you. Let not your heart be troubled, neither let it be afraid.

JOHN 14:27 KJV

Final Words of Encouragement

Experience life to the fullest. Live every day like it was your last day! Each day is a gift from God. With this gift, we must learn to *love* more, *laugh* vigorously, and *live* life knowing that tomorrow is not promised. Yes, things will happen, but we must be faithful to endure.

> *Blessed is the man that endureth temptation: for when he is tried, he shall receive the crown of life, which the Lord hath promised to them that love him.*

> — James 1:12 KJV

About the Author

Sophia McCray is native-born to the island of Bermuda. She now lives in Maryland and has a passion for writing and music. Sophia is a mom of two boys. She uses her personal life experiences to make her writing come alive. Living on faith and the Word of God, Sophia believes that transparency is the key to becoming a successful writer.

www.ingramcontent.com/pod-product-compliance
Lightning Source LLC
Chambersburg PA
CBHW071021120626
46546CB00003B/1188